Life around the World
Christmas in Many Cultures

by Martha E. H. Rustad

Consulting Editor: Gail Saunders-Smith, PhD

Capstone press

Mankato, Minnesota

Pebble Plus is published by Capstone Press,
151 Good Counsel Drive, P.O. Box 669, Mankato, Minnesota 56002.
www.capstonepress.com

1 2 3 4 5 6 13 12 11 10 09 08

Library of Congress Cataloging-in-Publication Data
Rustad, Martha E. H. (Martha Elizabeth Hillman), 1975–
     Christmas in many cultures / by Martha E. H. Rustad.
     p. cm. — (Pebble plus. Life around the world)
     Summary: "Simple text and photographs present Christmas in many cultures" — Provided by publisher.
     Includes bibliographical references and index.
     ISBN-13: 978-1-4296-1742-0 (hardcover)
     ISBN-10: 1-4296-1742-X (hardcover)
     1. Christmas — Juvenile literature. I. Title. II. Series.
GT4985.5.R87 2009
394.2663 — dc22   2008004187

Editorial Credits
Sarah L. Schuette, editor; Kim Brown, book designer; Alison Thiele, set designer; Wanda Winch, photo researcher

Photo Credits
Alamy/Images of Africa Photobank/Friedrich von Horsten, 17
AP Images/Teh Eng Koon, 11
Art Directors & Trip/Dimitri Mossienko, 7
Capstone Press/Karon Dubke, cover, 1, 21
Corbis/The Cover Story/Floris Leeuwenberg, 13; Godong/Thierry Bresillon, 15
The Image Works/Harriet Gans, 5
Landov LLC/Reuters/David Gray, 19
Peter Arnold/Paul O. Boisvert, 9

Note to Parents and Teachers

The Life around the World set supports national social studies standards related to
culture and geography. This book describes and illustrates Christmas in many cultures.
The images support early readers in understanding the text. The repetition of words and
phrases helps early readers learn new words. This book also introduces early readers
to subject-specific vocabulary words, which are defined in the Glossary section. Early
readers may need assistance to read some words and to use the Table of Contents,
Glossary, Read More, Internet Sites, and Index sections of the book.

Table of Contents

Christmas

People celebrate Christmas
in many cultures.
How are your Christmas
traditions like those
in other countries?

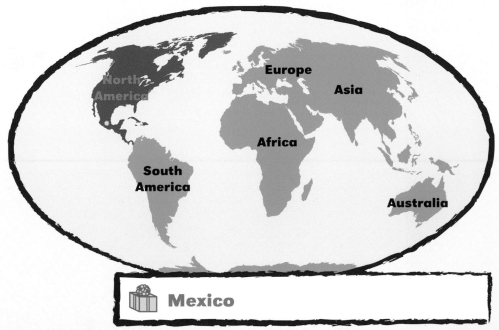

Mexico

Getting Ready

People cook special food
for Christmas.

A woman in the Ukraine
bakes bread.

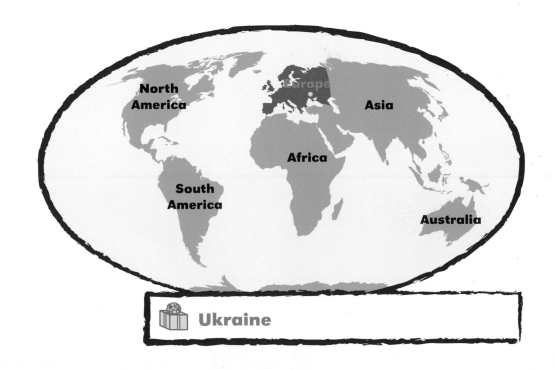

Ukraine

People put up

Christmas trees.

A family in the United States

finds a tree to take home.

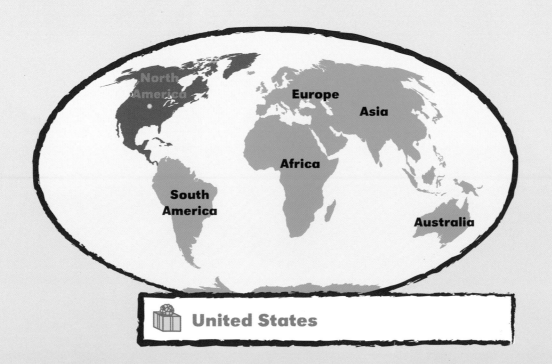

United States

8

Dressing Up

People dress up in costumes

for Christmas.

Children in Malaysia dress up

like Santa Claus.

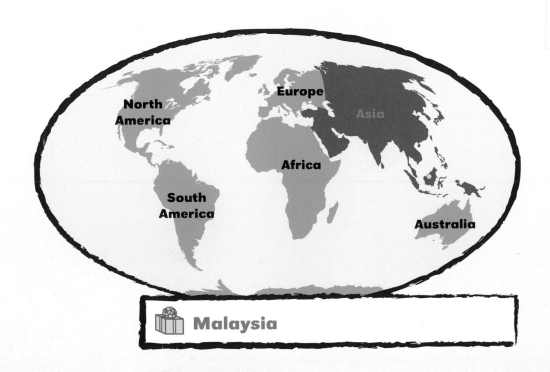

Malaysia

People dress up
for Christmas parties.
Children in Iceland dress up
in colorful costumes.

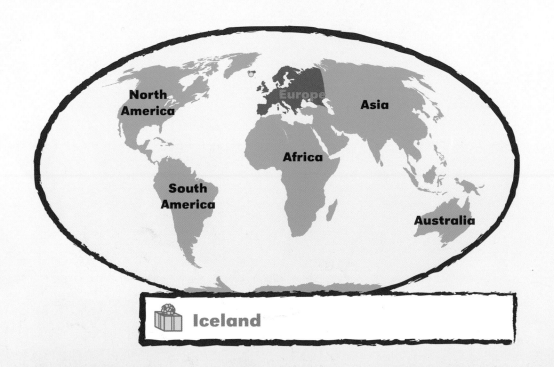

North
America

Europe

Asia

Africa

South
America

Australia

Iceland

People in Ethiopia wear colorful Christmas gowns as they walk to church.

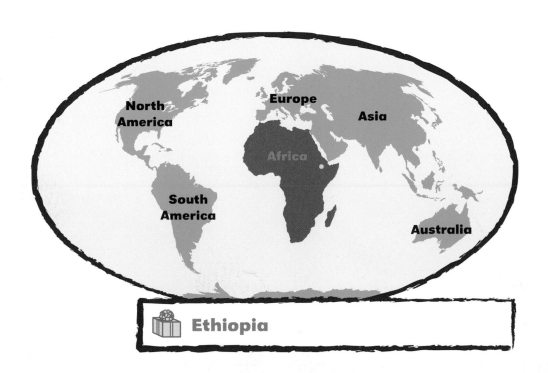

Ethiopia

Christmas Fun

People in South Africa
watch the sunrise
on Christmas morning.

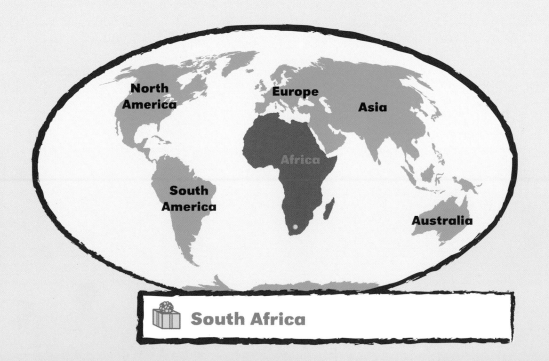

South Africa

People in Australia
go to the beach
on Christmas Day.

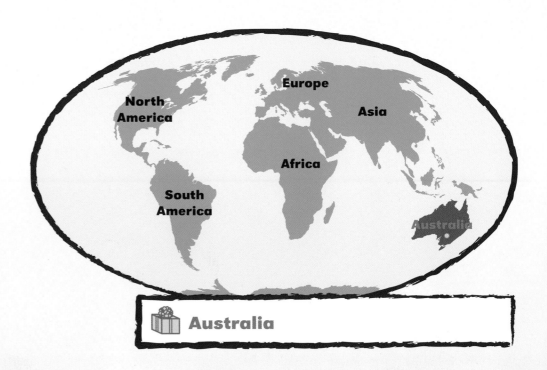

Australia

19

Around the world,

people sing, give gifts,

and eat treats at Christmas.

What will you do

for Christmas?

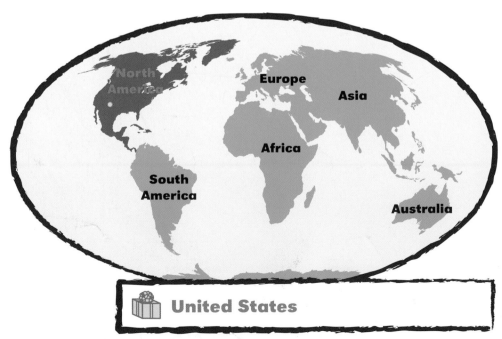

North America

Europe

Asia

Africa

South America

Australia

United States

Glossary

celebrate — to do something fun on a special day

costume — clothes worn by people dressing in disguise or for an event

culture — the way of life, ideas, customs, and traditions of a group of people

gown — a loose robe

tradition — a custom, idea, or belief that is handed down from one generation to the next

Read More

Heiligman, Deborah. *Celebrate Christmas.* Holidays around the World. Washington, D.C.: National Geographic, 2007.

Powell, Jillian. *Christmas.* Why Is This Festival Special? North Mankato, Minn.: Smart Apple Media, 2007.

Trueit, Trudi Strain. *Christmas.* Holidays, Festivals, and Celebrations. Mankato, Minn.: Child's World, 2008.

Internet Sites

FactHound offers a safe, fun way to find Internet sites related to this book. All of the sites on FactHound have been researched by our staff.

Here's how:

1. Visit *www.facthound.com*

2. Choose your grade level.

3. Type in this book ID **142961742X** for age-appropriate sites. You may also browse subjects by clicking on letters, or by clicking on pictures and words.

4. Click on the **Fetch It** button.

FactHound will fetch the best sites for you!

Index

Word Count: 125
Grade: 1
Early-Intervention Level: 18